Emotional Turmoil Comedy for Gay Lovers Pt II

Maverick Ashley Lenartson, Ph.D. Filthology

<u>Hint</u>: in order to become a lousier, i.e., better Comedian you have to <u>practice</u>, <u>practice</u>, <u>and practice</u> your comedy all the time and listen to the tapes you make in a recorder or that you write down on a 3X5 Card. You can choose from Physical Comedy, Stand Up Comedy w/ a 3X5 Card or Improvisation (making stuff up on the spot) or any other kind of comedy that is preferably <u>memorized</u>. Committing your comedy to <u>memory</u> means that you really did something good as you can't screw it up unless of course you get drunk, high or distracted before the show happens. BAD IDEA: Stay Sober and have a drink of whatever beverage you like drinking AFTER THE SHOW HAPPENS: that's your REWARD FOR DOING A LOUSY or GREAT JOB. Make sure that before you decide to show up to a Comedy Club that you know the following: Comedy Clubs & Comedians who run show <u>DISCRIMINATE</u> AGAINST EVERYBODY & find out what the <u>RULES</u> are before you decide to just show up out of the blue: it pays to be prepared in advance of showing up expecting to get put on the stage. That just won't cut it. You have to practice your "unfunny" comedy any chance you get and just because a joke worked in one club doesn't mean that it's going to work in another club as the night always changes and so do the clientele that go to Comedy Clubs all over the world. Being a "Comedian" is like a 'One Nite Stand' every time you go: <u>your funny/fun loving lover is your audience</u>. It's up to you to write or find jokes that you've rehearsed in front of people so you can know what does and doesn't work. Practicing your craft is like learning how to create a "Craft Beer", to make a cabinet or learning how to sing on key thru a broken nose. <u>REMEMBER</u>: your "Comedy Career" is not going to become a career in the finest sense of the words written here unless it's meant to be. You want to get paid for your comedy: write a book, make an Audio Book or bring a hat or sand pail with you when you perform your act and hand it out to any Audience Member, not the person ruining the show, I mean running the show. Chances are that the person who is running the "Comedy Show" that night is <u>being paid</u> by the owner of the bar/club/venue or at the very least the person who is running the bar for the evening. It's best to focus on becoming an "Amateur Comedian" and not a "Professional Stand Up Comedian" as that implies your being <u>PAID</u> regularly and you know that isn't

happening anytime soon unless you follow what I just wrote a few sentences back about getting paid for your hard earned writing and Potty Mouth, i.e., diarrhea of the potty mouth; coming up with a set list that you know works for you and not necessarily your audience is what you need to do. Not everybody is meant succeed all the time: that's the beauty of being a "Stand-Up Comedian": you get to keep doing it when there are shows available and practicing your craft is what's going to get you <u>INVITED TO OTHER COMEDY CLUBS OUTSIDE OF WHEREVER YOU LIVE</u>. When you fail miserably with your material just remember that you can always break out the worst joke in the world: it's called 'The Aristocrats Joke': throw that at your audience in a really high pitched voice: make it sound like you had sex w/ your whole family in any way, shape or form to bring your audience back to listening to you and you will become a successful comedian. Make sure that you moan and groan as the Audience is <u>GUARANTEED TO LAUGH NO MATTER WHAT</u>. Remember that after you have brought out this "little shop of horrors story/joke" that your audience is going to really want to "kill" your comedy set so make sure that you get back to your "Set List" and give it all you've got. That's the Rule #1. **RULE #1** <u>SECRET</u> to becoming a good comedian: keep failing until you get what you want out of speaking to an audience and making them laugh when you do your "Comedy Sets". Eventually, you will get really good at being a sucksexful (successful) comedian: It's not that your material sucks: did you ever think that you suck at being funny and that's why you want to become a successful comedian??? You have a major case of low-self-esteem & the best thing you can do here is: <u>Forget About having Low-Self Esteem</u>: sublimate your darn <u>EGO</u> and live your life anyways: that's why you are <u>HERE NOW</u> reading this book. You don't like this book or your life??? It could be 50++ Times WORSE: Become a Grateful Person: The <u>ONLY</u> Person responsible for making you funny is <u>YOU</u>: sweet, wonderful you. You can always give this unfunny comedy book to somebody as a gift to somebody that you like or don't like: then the book will end up in somebody else's hands and they'll read it and laugh their a** off…Keep Sucking Because You Can Only Suck For So Long and then you will become a "good successful" Stand-Up Comedian at some point in the game: making people laugh is no easy feat: you just have to keep trying until you succeed at being the funny person you know yourself to be: you are going to have good nights and bad nights as a "Stand-Up Comedian" and sometimes what you think is funny won't be funny at all and you're going to completely bomb in front of your audience. That's 'The Death of a Comedian': All "Comedy Clubs" or "Amateur Nights" <u>DISCRIMINATE AGAINST COMEDIANS</u>: this is the kind of world we live in all things being UNEQUAL.

'every successful comedian in the world has their good nights and their bad nights'. That's the life of a Stand-Up Comedian. Don't let that bother you. **RULE #2** about becoming a good comedian: if all else has failed and you know that you suck at being a Comedian you can always yell everything at your Audience as then you are <u>GUARANTEED TO MAKE YOUR AUDIENCE LAUGH</u>: it won't matter what you are saying because the audience is going to think that you are pissed off at the world and that isn't such a bad place to be in now is it? It works for <u>**Lewis Black**</u>: he always sounds like he's having a '**Bad Life**' and like he's going to have a heart attack or something worse. You can also buy a book thru Amazon or any other site about how to become a Successful Comedian in the World of Comedian as there are millions of starving comedians out there: the goal is to compete w/ yourself and not the comedians you are "up against". Remember that you are just trying to make people laugh in a world full of haters, masturbators and what not. You can also hang out with a group of Comedians by taking "A Course in Comedy Miracles" for 300 and you'll get 9 classes and get a "Certificate in Comedy". Not such a bad idea when you want to pay to learn the secrets of becoming a funny successful comedian in a cut-throat world of mercenaries who don't give a rats ass if you succeed or fail trying to be funny: it's all on you and I Believe In Your Ability To Become FUNNY: break a leg if you must. Eventually, persistence will pay off and you will break through to being a funny comedian. It's only a matter of time when that happens. **RULE #3**: Make sure that you laugh 50++ Times Per Day to keep up the dopamine levels you need in your body so that you can keep being a Funny Man or a Funny Woman…Rule #4: Buy this book, come up with a comedy set based on what I wrote for the jokes that appeal to you like a slippery banana and use these jokes in your Comedy Act. How am I going to know that you stole my BEST MATERIAL??? I won't and I give you complete permission to do this. Also, buying this book to use in your "Stand-Up/Improvisation Comedy Act" is a start. **RULE #4**: If you want to talk dirty to people you can do that but don't do it unless you ask the person or people you are with if they want you to talk like that to them. As a rule, when you sign up for "Amateur Comedy" at a Comedy Club you have to keep the swear words out of your Act as Comedy Clubs won't tell you this #1 RULE: "We are a family inclusive club and we discriminate against everybody. We're just not going to tell you that. It's up to you to find out what the rules of the Comedy Club are before you get there and not show up unannounced as you won't be able to get On Stage as everything is done upfront and before you get there. And like people keep saying to you, "Good Luck," & "Break a Leg." Comedy is all about being an

Adult & being funny. Work on your Act, give it a name and polish it until it shines britely like you do. That's the BEST that you can do!!!

Biff Barnaby = one of my porn names or a sleuth

Life Is Fun when you are on alcohol, marijuana, pills or food: Get High!!!

Prozac = the last time I stole a friends medication I wanted to kill people for two days after taking it

Lithium is made for batteries. Why would you want to put that into a person?

Haldol = anybody ever heard of the Haldol shuffle??? The only reason I know of the "Haldol shuffle" is because I once got admitted to MMC here in Portland, Maine for two weeks and my doctor was Dr. Colon Pope so I said to him one day when I was supposed to speak to him, "So, you're the pope with no hope." He said, "Excuse me." I said, "Just forget what I said." Then the appointment continued on. Remember, you don't need to put extra dopamine in your system as it will make you depressed and suicidal when you stop taking it. Just remember to laugh about your being NEUROTIC and to crack as many jokes as you can or to look in the mirror when you are naked or not naked and laugh as much as you can: you'll feel better from increasing your serotonin levels naturally!!!

Heroin = That's the only drug that can motivate me to do anything: anybody got any heroin???

I need downers to calm me down, not uppers to calm me up

I hired a new maid who's completely stupid and only listens to my slumlord, Donald W.F. All he ever says is, "Yessa Massa, Yes sa," or, "I only does what you tells me to do Massa." He just looks at her and laughs in his face.

Needs: friendlier, less fucked up tenants if one is to own a house or rooming house.

A warmer client to live in: that's what I could use: who needs to freeze their arse off for roughly 6 months of the year??? I surely don't. A place where the skies are not cloudy all day!

More money: who doesn't like having more money in their life? As in Mo Money!

A newer house to live in. I just love that fresh house smell like when I buy a new house to live in with C.A.S.H.

Less Ignorant Maine Residents: there are too many people out there with 5th Grade Edjewmuhcaytions: that's all I can say.

People who actually pay attention and who don't say **"YES"** just to say 'YES'. I'm now a **NO MAN**. I like saying **NO** to addicts. I don't need any more addicts in my life. And, when they persist, I like to say, "Go Love Your Self." They say, "Excuse Me." I say, "Go Lover Your Self." They say, "Did you just tell me to go fuck myself." I say, "If that's what you think I just told you then yes, I did tell you to go love yourself."

COMEDY – MAKING TRACKS

Walk on stage: crooked gait. I bet you thought I was suffering from some malady didn't you? I just wanted to observe how gullible some of your people are!!!!!!!!!!!!

Crazy people = "The Crazy Lady". Whatever happened to the crazy lady down the road??? She finally died from being & acting crazy. She just couldn't help herself.

Snack Ramen Noodles = MSG is like a drug as it makes you high and gives you hives and a headache. What's up with that??? If you want to get high w/ the side FX then go ahead and put a package of snack ramen noodle flavoring in a hot cuppa water and drink it on down when it cools. Who would have thunk it???

Squirrel Talk = I have a friend by the name of Lorin Ginn who likes to speak in squirrel talk. She used to have a squirrely boyfriend but they broke up for some strange reason. His name was Doug Palmer.

Manic Depression/Bi-Polar = I have a mental health issue. I don't see it as a barrier to living my life. I'm actually a Bi Polar Bear who lives in Portland, Maine. I like having sex with other bi-polar bears as I'm 55 years older, not younger & I'm gaining weight on account of my age and eating too much food. What a pig I have become.

Schizophrenic people are very smart people. You have to watch out for them as they will best you most of the time.

Drink 6-8 cups of really fine Brazilian **Coffee** before going to bed. Find out what happens besides not being able to sleep. You are going to turn into a Psychic and pick up the negative energy that people throw out at each other and lock yourself away in your room if you can. You'll be imagining all sorts of negative things happening to you. It's not going to be pretty.

Michael Jackson = I really don't know what the hell happened to him. He definitely turned into a freakazoid. His "negative karma" started happening to him when that accident happened while he was filming that Pepsi Commercial which never got aired on account of his hair catching on fire during the filming of the commercial. That's when the doctor prescribed him pain pills for his burnt scalp.

Drinking – If I'm going to be drinking alcohol-uh-I usually don't drink-well then I like to slam it down very quickly. Like the time I celebrated with employees when I used to work @Boone's Restaurant on Commercial Street. Alcohol makes me do things I usually don't do. Feeling up a female, bending over and feeling like Rover, driving my bicycle home drunk weaving from right to left on the road being careful not to cross the yellow line on Congress Street. What's up with THAT???

Going to a bar and drinking Bud Light Beers – It's alright but since I bought pitchers of it and had not drunk beer for a while, I sucked the beer straight from the pitcher all in a matter of 1 ½ hours and proceeded to leave the bar feeling very good about myself. I like that fact that I don't get nasty when I drink beer in public. I turn into a happy drunk. I'm very lucky there.

Miller Light – It's piss beer. It may have a golden look and flavor but the best part about drinking any piss beer is the head the beer gives me. I never thought it was possible to get head from beer but it sure is possible: **foam**. Want more foam in your beer: pour table salt in your beer. Mix the beer with your spoon or chopstick and all that head magically appears. Next time you need a little bit of head, drink some beer. The beer takes the place of the woman. Miller Light doesn't smell like piss, but the color and the taste sure do remind me of piss because it's golden in color which is the prize of making the beer. Of course, if you like drinking piss well then you are all set. That's your kind of beer, not mine. Of course, if you happen to be **GAY** and like drinking piss, nah—forget I said that. I don't want to insult more than half of my audience tonight.

Just because a straight man likes to suck cock and take it up the ass doesn't mean that he is **GAY**. It just means that he's a **COCKSUCKER** & he has a mangina between his legs. Just don't ask him if he is **GAY**! Ask him about his girlfriend and I they're having great sex and how the weather is...

ASS SNIFFER: are there any ass sniffers in the audience tonight???

Future Jokes: what are jokes from the future: **IMPROVISATION**!

I told my mom to have a conversation with her relatives, her mother, father and brother. What's up with that??? They're all dead...

The Tobin Bridge – who doesn't like being in the middle of a bridge during Rush Hour trying to get a ride back to Maine with a whole bunch of supplies in their hands???

Answering Machine Messages: weird calls in the middle of the night or at any other time of the day. What's up with that??? Some people just don't know when to call during the day. I can see calling in the middle of the night if you know that's when you are supposed to call somebody up but otherwise, why do it??? That's why I keep a whistle around my neck so I can really let them have it.

Stupid Human Tricks. How many times can you say, "Hi," in one day and someone says, "Not!" or nothing. They don't even smile at you. Baby, same shit, different day. Wouldn't it be nice if someone said, "I'm Ecstatic." That would be nice to hear.

<u>Jokes for Gay People</u>

Cream of Sperm Soup from Campbell's

The Sperm Burgler from McBungholes Restaurant

The Sperm Burper Highway by I.M. Harder

Sperm Drop Cookies

Sperm Drop Candy

I'm the middle child. No wonder I need attention all the time. I'm the stupid one according to my parents but I'm simply not buying that anymore. Thank God I'm not being verbally and physically abused anymore. I'm a **FREE MAN**!!!

Thank God Daddy Didn't Pull Out In Time or I wouldn't be here!!!

My Mamas Better Than Your Mama

My Papas Better Than Your Papa

Off Like a Prom dress

Excellent = Egg sell ent

Surprised = Slurprised

Business = Bizznass

What's Up!!! What??? All of a sudden you're black???

What's up with raising a boy as a girl? Or, a girl as a boy??? Talk about being confused later on in life and hating anything that is the opposite sex you are.

Soft, Easy & Refreshing: my bf or gf

Forgive Your Self: that's the only person you can forgive and, all of the people who have fuct you over in this lifetime and all the people you've gotten even with because they deserved it!!!

Women are only good for sucking the money out of my bank account, having children and throwing me in jail because anybody with a brain knows that women have all the rights in Society, not men, so you must be very careful when dealing with some woah!men. Some men as well.

My favorite movie of all time is **HOMO ALONE**

I'm related to **Deep Throat**...he's my brother...

You have to be your own best friend: best friends are very hard to keep & they usually want favors from you as they're too lazy to do whatever it is that they need to do on their own without a small loan, to borrow something from you that they don't return or to talk your ears off.

I already got off as I'm not waiting for Mr. Right to show up as he's usually Mr. Wrong: Been there, Done that!!! Next, I said, "Next."

Ronald Morris
Was in an auto accident but ok thanks for asking
Ashley Lenartson
you can use **Ben Gay** on it and he'll make you feel better...ha ha ha ha ha ha ha...I know, I know...I just made a joke

lots of loads, lots and lots and lots of white creamy dreamy loads of icing on the green cake Donna Summers sings about in that hugely popular song, "MacArthur Park".

Big Wood is the name of my new rock band or **Big Woody**

William Davis
Yum buddy, wanna give me some…
Maverick Ashley Lenartson
I'll bake a cake and put jizz in the icing for you.
William Davis
Down with the batter, I got the recipe
Maverick Ashley Lenartson
I know what the recipe requires
William Davis

How long to bake

Maverick Ashley Lenartson

I'll cum over to your house, whip out my dick, you start sucking me off: no muss, no fuss: it'll take as long as you like for the white icing to come out…you'll know when I'm done and your mouth is full of white icing…will that make you happier??? I sure hope so…

William Davis

I'll clean the house first, then I'll blow you

Maverick Ashley Lenartson

Don't bother cleaning the house: I've experienced worse trauma in my lifetime: not a big deal if your house is messy. You can clean it up after I leave.

William Davis

Oh wait, the cake

Maverick Ashley Lenartson

The cake has green icing and it's sitting in MacArthur Park

William Davis

Candy, raining in the dark, lol, you're a lot of fun

Maverick Ashley Lenartson

I know, I know…I'm a Cumedian…

William Davis

Yum hun. Lick it up!

Maverick Ashley Lenartson

That's it get all the green icing down your throat and tell me to bake another cake with green icing in MacArthur Park

William Davis

We could play well together
You'll say something & I'll twist it ever so

Maverick Ashley Lenartson

Some people say I have a "sick mind" but I don't pay no heed to them: they just don't understand the mind of a twisted comic…I go from one topic to the next topic…I'm not an actor, I'm a seductive actress: I use words to seduce my audience. If one says I'm "sick" that means there's a cure: I'm not interested in being "cured".

William Davis

I'm a single sick fucka. It's all in my head

Maverick Ashley Lenartson

you mean mutha fucka...that's right, I had sex w/ my whole family - The Aristocrats

And have a heart of gold and I'll still fucka you!
Mousecowits

Have fun doing that

Ahh, you're great: gotta go for now

Thanks for the cumpliment

I gotta go, ttyl

have a great evening...be kind to your self

You as well, Sir!

Is that thumb going up my ass??? I sure hope so…

No, it's my tongue, then it's my thumb

Open up that hole like only you can

I wish I could lick my own asshole...or suck my dick all the way to the base
& cum in my hot dirty purty little hot mouth...

I sat on my face...and I farted but it was more than a fart...I had to stop the
avalanche from coming out...so, I put my fist up there...

You have to ask yourself why you keep being mean to yourself: it's always
Ego related: you'll get an answer you may not like!

who wants to see me take off all my clothes and run down the street
NAKED???

It's going to be a laugh fest, that's fer sher...

When somebody says, "Hi" to me why are they asking me if I'm high???

Don't ask me how I'm doing unless you have some really good drugs like weed, alcohol, food or you to get high off of…

Why not have a good time all the time???

Why is it when I send naked pix of me to someone online they say, "You?" I say, "No, it's my brother or my sister: she has a penis."

I want to go to an **Orgy** and be the center of all the attention and get cream pied by a bunch of different guys and gals.

Emillio
You're hot
Maverick Ashley Lenartson
I'm hotter in person

Ronald Sinkler
You going to fuck me hard???
Maverick Ashley Lenartson
I'm going to fuck you so hard and cum in your ass. Then I'm going to tell you to push it out of your asshole and lick it up like an ice cream cone…

The Cocksuckers Association: who wants to join???

Hey there 'Orgy Boy', will you suck my dick off??? Give it to me now!

I live at **The Island of Forgotten Toys, Portland, Maine**

<u>DeVos wants to change campus rules on sexual misconduct</u>

Remember: a man or a woman can say, "He/She raped me," and you never laid a hand on that person or, maybe, you manhandled that person: **manhandling** a person is different from raping them as one is **BDSM** and the other is <u>'forcing your way into or on a person'</u>...two separate ideas...be careful who you "**sexually harass these days**"...it could wind up becoming "downright dirty, dirty, dirty to the bone" w/ the "he said, she said" shite...it happened to me once: thank god the woman I was seeing at the time decided not to call the **<u>Police</u>** as I would have been in knee deep doo-doo and she's no longer my friend: she passed from "brain cancer" as she was susceptible to Cancer...not my fault...I got her to apologize in front of 3 witnesses but she wouldn't look me in the eyes and that pissed me off even further but at least I got a "forced apology out of her" in front of people as I have no interest in "raping a 73 year older woman or man for that matter." It's not my style.

Fuck It Like It's Hot: Doc Johnson gets the job done for as long as you need and he's not going to say, "Honey, I've got a headache," or "Not tonight honey because I don't feel like it." He always comes thru for me!!!

Suck It Like It's Hot: what am I sucking: hell to the No!!!

Make Love To The Whole Wide World: nothing can bring you down ever except your negative thoughts & that's your living **HELL**!!!

What's your name: who's asking or Ha! Ha! Or Ha ha ha ha ha ha ha…

I don't need a Daddy as I am the Daddy: my names **Daddalicious**

Have a great evening everybody: time to get off facebook

Why did the penis get limp? It was suffering from organ failure

IBM Card Wreaths for Veterans: 93.90 each: I'll give you a fun Blue or Red Lobstah Shirt just for buying the wreath as a **BONEUS**: 34.60 values...that's a **VALUE** of 138.50 for 93.90 thanks so much...Happy Holidays...Gobble! Gobble! Sir Maverick Ashley Lenartson 198 Sherwood St 3 Portland, Maine 04103 207-450-3140

John West
On a farm. Ok good, love it. Do you work on a farm or you bought the farm because you are a farmer? I dunno. Ha ha. John West I'm a farmer with my brothers: I love it. I don't do anything. I watch. I was an accident.

Why are **pencils** called colored pencils??? Because they like to make things that are colorful & that brighten anybody's day!!!

<u>'Come back dressed like a man.' Pastor recounts his confrontation with person dressed in 'drag' on Facebook Live.</u>

I can't stop laughing: what is "inappropriate dressing"??? Hmm… Pastor Antonio Rocquemore of Power House International Ministries

I lost my hands from masturbating too much: I had to have the surgery for using them too much as they were starting to atrophy and the surgery didn't take so I'm handless: can anybody give me a hand here??? Thanks so much

I only jerk off one time a year and cover the whole nayborehood in snow...

No Christmas shopping for me: all I have to do is look thru my apartment and find stuff I don't want: it works like a charm every year.

My hole is twitching right now: I think it's going to suck your tongue, fingers, fist or dick in it

What do you do when your hole twitches??? I wipe mine or scratch mine

What's your **birth sign**: Crazy

I put it in very **slowly** like a turtle then I fuck like Bugs Bunny!!!

Sounds like a **triple orgasm**: if you are a multiple-cummer? Hell to the **NO**!!! If I was a multiple-cummer then that would mean that my body is anticipating the idea of cumming and that's just the way it is: you can use coffee, pot, beer, a cockring, thick rubberbands or your tight hands to make you not cummmmm or to hold back the impending orgasm that's going to embareass you….

I'm related to Porky Pig right now butt eye'm ok w/ that...

How do you purse your lips??? I pull down my pants and spread my ass cheeks so you can get a very good look at my other mouth...be careful as there are teeth in my asshole...the same thing goes for a woman's pussy: make sure that you never go there w/ a person unless the teeth have been disabled!!!

I'm in a relationship right now: I'm seeing my friend <u>Doc Johnson</u>: he really loves me and never says **NO**...or, "Honey, I've got a headache."

I was 4 lbs...in an incubator for x amount of days, weeks & months: no wonder my cock is so big: it got too much Oxygen...

I love to lay NAKED outdoors but only 10 minutes...you mite miss me when I do make an appearance in public.

A friend of mine told me not to pierce my nipples so I pierced his nipples. Now he feels like a woman.

Yuh. Move out of Maine. Nothing here except good scenery, backward woods country, Maine girls are crazy here. Guys are, too! So basically everybody here in Maine is **CRAZY**. What's left???

The Muppet Master = The Puppet Master. My friend 'Chrissy Snow' told me that, "You are the puppet master." Anybody want me to put my hand up their ass and make them say things they wouldn't normally say???

I shit my diaper: I did it on purpose. People could smell the stink of my diapers but I didn't say anything. I was eating at a restaurant eating dinner.

I need a **ball gag** in my mouth. Does anyone have a **ball gag**???

Stay out of the son unless he cums in your buns, stay away from the heat unless you like the hot meat, don't do anything unless it makes you feel cumplete...

Just found out I'm pregnant, going to have a baby girlll. Have a slappy day with your clients. Moe's a hot pig! I've lost 235lbs: I divorced my husband! Help the Homeless: throw your spare change on the sidewalk when they ask for it!!! Have more ████████ with your life: ask me how!!! You are a beautiful Pillsbury Dough Girl!!! What kind of sex do bears have? Bearback. Have you seen 'Casper the Friendly Ghost'? Neither have I. Orange you glad to see me said the orange to the grape??? The grape replied, "I'm so grapeful" I said, "I'm fruit loop. I'm related to fruit poop. He's my stinky brother." I'm the Other White Meat now that Michael Jackson's gone!!! If it's before 8 it's too late. Get me higher than a kite, Lisa. I'm wealthy: Congrat U Lay tions, You're a Weener!!! What did the cow get caught for??? A mooving violation. The Purple Cow, how may I help you??? Mike Hawk married Mike Hunt. They had a child they named him Hawk Hunter. Say "Marry Christmas & Happy Halloween every day when it isn't the holiday season." I just got a new job: I'm working Mellen and Deering Streets. I'm a hooker. I like to make rugs. Everybody is a prostitute for something as they sell themselves every day of the year. Don't deny it. Just admit it. We're all "**Prostitutes from Prostitutionland**".

Yeah Rite! You are a valuable Ass!etc. of the company beatch! I'd shit myself on purpose just to piss off **the Boss**, just to say that I did it. Personally. He's not going to be firing anybody. He's going to get mad and make you change your diaper. He's just a miserable person. Crack some filthy jokes or some **PG-Rated Jokes** to find out if he has any sense of humor. He's the Boss of the cumpany. He can act anyway he pleases as it's his company. He likes people who do their jobs that are assigned to them. He doesn't like anybody that deviates from his usual method of business. That's his job. That's why he's an asshole. He's like most people I've met in my lifetime: an asshole. Welcome to Assholville, Maine, how can I help you???

I told my good friend, Brion J., to piss off his boss by shitting in his diaper. I said, "When you do it you must say, "I didn't shit myself. It must be something coming into the vehicle." He didn't do it. He should have. I would have. I also told Brion, "You are a pussy anyways: an ass **kisser**. Suit yourself."

I'm your **Puppet Master**: You do as you are told: Piss your Boss off or I'm going to personally call him up and tell him about your behavior lately. I don't like your attitude. It sucks. It's bringing down the whole company. You must be a team player and sometimes it's good to piss off the Boss. Besides, when you do it it's good for the morale of the company. It really IS...gives people something to talk about and for them to wonder what you're going to do next!!!

Show me the **proof**: The proofs in the **putentane**.

I'm **Sasquatch**: please ta meat ya! I live @ Washingzoo Gardens, Portland, Maine

Impeccable = Im pecker able

I went to the doctor the other day: He gave me an **Rx**: "Nuts Just Plain Nuts". I told him, "I'm not paying the bill." It was the end of that session. I told him I'm a bird and flew away. He didn't know what to say.

I didn't know that you were **shitfucking** your boss. How cum you didn't tell me??? I'm going to have to shave my armpits today as I'm sick of the underarm hair bugging me...

Next time you cum over bring your doctors bag for a long session: the cockpump, nipple clamps, anything else you can think of just bring it with you and bring Ron, as well! Ask him when he's free to meat me...I mean meet so we can get better acquainted with each other.

Carolyn is a **<u>Nasty Older Troll</u>** who is totally into her **self**: a fuddy duddy who goes on and on and on and on, has boundary issues like her mouthy son who I'd love to suck off and bend over for: it would be NASTY! As he looks like a nut job just like she is. I should ask him when he wants a back massage; see what his response is...

My dream boat   lover. Who here is looking for a dream boat banana lover??? Anybody???

Hot Boys Walking @ The Fryberg Fair

Hot Girls Walking @ The Fryberg Fair

My new buttfuckee boyfriend: could be anybody that can last for as little as 30 seconds

Something for you to suck on: a   **nipple**

The **Mad Scientist**: what makes him so mad anyways??? He doesn't have much of a sense of humor. The most important thing about being a Mad Scientist IS developing his or her sense of humor.

I'd Eat Him Out: anybody here want to get eaten out in a back alleyway after this book is finished or read at a Gay bar in Portland, Maine??? Come on, don't be shy…

I'm an Expert @ diffusing big bombs, really big bombs. Make sure that the next time you fart to close all the windows in the vicinity of the fart. It's going to be more fragrant. You might even make somebody throw up from the fumes of the fart. That's what Huey Lewis of Huey Lewis & The News does.

I like   my farts. Don't deny it. You like doing it too!!! Only a woah!man would deny that they even have a fart box btwn their legs. Remember, women are supposed to docile & express themselves. Men are supposed to be hostile and not express themselves: no wonder the world is fuct up!!!

My naybore @ Troll Island. She looks like a Troll with her bugeyes: she's Ultra Serious: has not much of a sense of humor like those Goonies in that movie that go **POOF!!!**

You're a Professional Liar, huh??? Happens to the best of US. Best to quit before you get Cancer from smoking huh??? Go see a Hypnotist. That's what I'd do. Go pack your poo poo bear!!!

I'm moving to   to have sex with bears. I'm into Bears now. When a bear shits in the woods, **_RUN_**…you are definitely much too close to the bear. Bears need **<u>PRIVACY</u>** anyways. They don't like being watched while they are taking a big nasty dump in the forest. Do you like being watched when you are on the toilet: question answered. In defense of the 21st Century: Big Brother is watching you no matter where you go so if you're going to be committing crimes makes sure that you come up w/ 25 reasons you will get caught committing that crime on camera: SMILE YOU ARE ON CANDID CAMERA!!!

Hey hose, No Way Hose! Be Swell Horni! I heart really big penises! FUN FUN FUN 'til daddy takes the T-Bird away! Aw Shit Fuck says Scarolyn, the ultra-serious shitkunt!

Wanna blow a hot creamy load all over my face, nut in my butt with a condom on it??? Happy Horni Spring: I'm into happeniss!!! Be swell, jerk one out for me. Laughter 50++ times per day: even if you can't think of anything funny to laugh about!!! Just do it for your own sanity!!!

Next time you cum over, you're going to have to take a dump in my terlit. Then I'm going to bang you very hard!

NAKED & AFRAID: That's YOU!!! I'd love to be on that show like going on "**Fear Factor**" but I'm not in shape and I'm over the age of 40. If you notice: everybody who goes on a reality show is usually in shape and they're less than the age of 40.

I'm ready fir anything, that's fur sure: you need somebody who's very hairy or who has no hair to ▓▓▓▓▓ with. I'd love to take care of my baby: you're my baby! **WA! WA! WA!**

That's going to be **FUN 'N HOTTER**: Get your taint done instead of having your ears or nipples pierced. Who's up for anus bleaching so that your next trick can't miss the target...?

My clothespins are on my nibs right now: they're very sore when I take them off. Gets those endorphins/serotonin going...who here doesn't like putting clothespins on their nipples and screaming out in pain as the endorphins get released and they make you feel better...

Anybody here ever been shit fucked??? I've done it to other guys and a few women: it's like a limo ride: it's FUN FUN FUN!!!

Anybody here want to take a dump on me? Just come up on stage. **NOT!** How about taking a piss all over me? I can get into the piss aspect but not the shit aspect as shit isn't my thing but I like a "golden shower" every now and then.

FACE THE MUSIC: You have a shitty job that you hate. Your boyfriend: he's a pussy. You get nervous when you speak in front of audiences. Your cat and dog left you, etc. You're truck's a pussy, your Boss is a pussy, employees are pussies,

Maine SUCKS ASS. I'm THE SUCKIEST PERSON YOU HAVE EVER MET! I'm a Major Pussy & you suck shitty butt when ordered to. What else IS NEW besides FAKE NEWS???!!!

When I grow up I'm going to be my elf, have fun being a **MANWHORE**. Loving every minute of it: "Can't get enough," said the Loverboy to his constituents.

Anybody here like paying for S-E-X: meat me after the show: I'll do you right like Kentucky Fried Chicken!!!

Find a **NEW MASTER** through the computer with a **WANT AD**: put an ad in the local gay bar!!! **WHAT I'D DO**. Figured out what to do about getting laid. Have **FUN** with your **LIFE**!

"Crank those orders out Aunt Jo Mama!!!" I said to my good friend, Michelle E. recently.

You're Rob is a bitch, your employer is a bitch, your employees are bitches, you're a bitch. Everybody is a bitch. Hell, I'm a bitch. We're all bitches. Speaking of bitches, here comes one right no.

Better start with a group that you can trust that you know of!!! Or, you could just go to Prison as then you are going to be somebody's bitch! Or...

All you have to do is find somebody to make you their bitch for the evening...

I just want a guy or a gal who wants to fuck me all night long and he wants to do it regularly. A boyfriend would be nice but I'm not holding my breath or counting any chickens...for some of us, having a relationship that works just doesn't work out in real life. That's just the way it is...scans the audience. Anybody here want to be my bitch??? I won't treat you like my bitch. I'll just call you dirty names when we have sex together. You ma'am...would you like to be my bitch??? How about you sir??? Anybody???

You are finished in Hollywood when you are over the age of 20 male or female. If you are over 40 and you are a woman forget about getting leading roles: That's a myth except for females. Unless you are a **Superstar** like Madonna, Cher or ME???

Have you been going to ballet or have you been blowing it off??? I wouldn't mind Rob pissing up my ass! A delivery driving job would be great for me but I'm vested in **Art**. That's the problem. Have to figure out a way to make a living from being a **Professional Artist**: that's my 'Profession in Life'.

At least you are working: I'm hardly working: well, actually, I'm working it!!!

Would you like to join The Meat Packers Union: We play the "Cornhole" Game? It's a FREE Game that is played out in the mid-west and is played with a tic-tac-toe board and a hacky sack filled with corn. Our other group is so much more fun to play as it allows for the freedom of expression: You can cornhole your partner and he or she's going to like it as they have no choice but to do it as they are told or **<u>GET THE FUCK OUT</u>** when they won't play that game!!!

Who wants to get **NAKED** right now??? Anybody??? Let's all take off our clothes right now and find out what happens.

Homo Phobia = a fear that you might actually like sucking a guy's cock and like it. You know, the last time you went out you got drunk and you sucked maybe 8, 9 guys off and you love it…it's amazing what can happen when you get drunk or baked and let your inhibitions go for the evening.

Embarrassment = Em bare ass ment: I like being em bare ass ed by my friends or somebody I don't even know

Step out of line and what happens: most of the time: **NOTHING**!!! **F E A R**

Carcass = Cark Ass. Get your cark ass over here right now!!!

Hot Bench = Hot Lunch = Hot Judge bent over the coffee table

Bear a ble = Bearable: let's make this trip bear able

When you put a bag over anyone's head that you don't like pictorially, then you can fuck them 6 ways to Sunday and more…it's amazing what a bag can do to somebody with making them look attractive. AMAZING!!! That's how I deal with people whose looks I don't like sexually speaking.

Hot Ghost Peppers = Hot Ghost Peckers: who's up for being fuct by Casper The Friendly Ghost??? Anybody??? OK, I'll go 1st.

Vagina = Mangina. Every guy has a mangina. He just doesn't know it yet.

Banana Split = Bone ana Split

What makes a man or a woman's' body parts more suckable: Whipped Cream, Honey, Chocolate Sauce and Strawberries. You don't need any nuts as the man you're doing it with either has nuts or is already nuts from loving you sexually speaking…he's hot for YOU!!!

Man Up & Be a Pussy with Your Boss = Just do your job or be prepared to get **FIRED**!!!

Who doesn't like saying these words: "**YOU'RE FIRED!!!**"

You're **Welcome** = You're Wel cum

Which tastes better: Asspussy, Ass or BOTH??? On a man or a woman or a Kaitlyn Jender Bender???!!! She claims to have had the surgery done but most of us will never know will we??? I think the best thing a person can be is transgender as people in the media are pushing for the rights of Transgender People here in America. I'd have a much better life IF I had a pussy between my legs. Then I'd be very unique and get all the hot meat I want from guys who like that sort of thing. Most guys would never consider fucking a guy unless he is wearing a dress.

I told my friend, Michelle Estell: "My assholes never been so raw in my whole life as Nate threw me to the ground last night and took me to Poundtown." He says, "You're NEXT!!!" Then I told her, "Nate's so rough, but so worth it." He's such a demanding pussy/lover but worth every penny I spent on him last night.

I told my friend, Brion, to shit his diaper on a trip he's taking with his boss to New Hampshire as he's urinary and fecal incontinent on account of his bladder issues & the doctor cutting the 'sacral nerve' in his butt. Just wait for the smell to waft through the vehicle and then tell him it was an accident!!! Get out of my truck!!!

Assessment = Ass ess ment

Life's Too Serious…to take anything ***SERIOUSLY***!!! Am I right, or am I right???!!!

It sure is very nice that I can talk to guys and chat them up and get exactly what women want from them: **A HOT LUNCH**. I ask them if there's anything they need like a beer, a joint, a cigarette, pills or money. I just love paying for **S-E-X** with guys I'm never going to ever see ever again in this 'One Horse Town' called Portland, Maine: why did I ever move here???!!! Oh, that's right: my twisted twin sistahh who thinks she's rich & black decided to move here in the early 80's. I should have opted to stay behind and let her move to Portland, Maine.

Who wants to join **The Meat Packers Union**: Membership is **FREE!!!**

Club 69 or **Club 13**: that was a club that two of my friends had started back in the early 90's…It was a **BDSM** Club: Bondage, Discipline, Sadism & Masochism. I got bored with being a **BDSM** Victim so I quit the club. Anybody here into serious **BDSM**? Meat me after the show. I think we can come to an agreement with you being my slave bitch.

Would anybody like to come over for a beer after the show??? We can talk about your life and see what happens next. I like beer, pot, pills and sex because they help me to relax and have a better time with whomever I am with…anybody? Ok, my telephone number is **450-3140: CALL ME**!!!

When I see shit on somebody's hole I simply wipe it away and start munching away…come to think of it, licking a little bit of shit on a guys' hole or even a woman's hole won't bother me at all as a little bit of shit never hurt anybody. It's good for your immune system when you think about shits' healing power. I'm not saying that I'm into shit but if the man or woman IS **HOT**, what's a little bit of shit in my life??? How could somebody even consider doing **THAT**???!!! **Just remember**: when you get stuck in the woods and begin to get hungry that your piss and your shit **IS** an option until help arrives. When help doesn't arrive all you have to do is go foraging for food in the woods or just find a good place to sit and set up camp for the night: Once you've got enough cover for the evening with your new shelter then you can start a fire and you can think about finding things to eat in the forest like cattail roots, pine tree roots or pine bark on a tree, berries off a bush, fiddleheads which grow near lakes, and so much more. Find a piece of glass and you've got a way to make a fire. Dig a hole and you can take a dump in it and then cover it up when you leave your camp. You can also make a cage out of pine boughs and weeds and then put that in the brook and see what kind of fish get trapped in the fish trap. There's so much that you can do to survive being lost in the Maine woods. When you remember, you can also find a metallic object so that you can flash it at the sun and somebody's going to realize that you are needing **H.E.L.P.** with being rescued when you flash out the letters S.O.S.= Shit on a Shingle. Oops! My Bad, I mean S.O.S. That would be three flashes of the S's and two flashes of the O's…you'll be rescued at some point. If you are stranded on a desert island then you're going to have to get used to being stranded and hope that a ship or airplane passes by and then you can use your glass or metallic object to get help if there is any to be found. I'd love to survive off of Nature but I'm too much of a pussy to actually do it. However, I think that IF I was forced into that situation for whatever reason, I'd find a way to survive and live to tell about it.

What exactly IS a Treasure Chest??? Anybody…OK, it's a porn store on Pine Street here in Portland, Maine. And, you can go in the back of the store and watch porn movies of every type and leave your door open and find out what happens next.

Retired = Retarded

I'm much too old to be Abused anymore. Therefore when somebody abuses me verbally I say to them, "Is that the best you can do??? Right now, you're trying to annoy me but it's not working." **Try HARDER**!!! Then start laughing at them when they continue on w/ their diatribe or wait until they're done.

Crazy = another word for somebody who is simply misunderstood by people and Society: now, if a person is insane in the membrain: **LOCK 'EM UP**!!!

Who would you rather have sex with: a padeophile or a peto phile??? I'd take NEITHER or NYTHER!!! That's my final offer. I'd rather pet my pet but not have sex with my pet.

Somebody asked me what kind of sex I like having: I told them I'm into cats, dogs, donkeys, cows and especially whales, horses & pigs…my sexuality is nobody's business but you know how inquiring minds want to know!!!

Secret Lover = My Blow Up Doll named Billy Blow Up or Betty Blow Up. I thought about buying a blow up sheep, cow or horse but I couldn't bring myself to blow the darn thing up when I brought it home so I gave it to my sister. She had no problem putting her mouth on the piece that helps you to get air inside the animal. My sister is so twisted that when I was younger I asked her to blow me up and she said, "YES." I politely declined that interaction. **The Aristocrats**. Speaking of Aristocrats: when the blue blood lines run out of people to continue on their blood lines they just bang each other to produce the next of kin. I know, I know…how could anyone even consider having sex with their distant cousin(s)??? I could do it as the distant cousin is far enough down the line to not affect the health of the baby from what I've learned. I could be wrong about what I'm saying but I just said it. It's **SHOCKING** to even hear!!!

Things that you bring to a **party**: a blindfold, a ball gage, rope, nipple clamps, boots, spit, dirty socks to shove in somebody's mouth, a room with a lightbulb in it, a Tazer or electric fly swatter, dirty underwear, used condoms, etc. All in a doctor's bag. Don't forget to stethoscope just in case anybody faints so you can find a heartbeat. And, smelling salts…just fill that doctors bag up with anything and everything that you can think of to bring with you.

Promises Promises Department, how can I help you???

I want to bend you over and put hot peppers and vicks vapo rub up your hole and then fuck the holy shit out of you honey. That's what I said to a good friend of mine who has mental health issues. Who doesn't have mental health issues? Anybody? That's why you are here: so I can make you forget about your problems.

My friend told me to go do what I have to do. I replied, "I'm going to 'F Myself, that's what I'm going to do. You should do that too as you're going to feel better Slave Brion."

My friend, Brion, shit his diaper so I said, "How'd it make you feel? SHITTY??? I think you should rub poison ivy all over your body. That'll make you happy. Put leeches in your crotch and watch them get bloated from drinking your blood. Those are things that he has done before. He's a little on the twisted side.

May as well squash it some more and make it give you a rash honey! You're a sensitive little boy r'nt ya! So am I! Have fun spontaneously shitting and pissing your pants **Professor Stinky Pants**.

Lick my asshole Mr. Bossman. Just do it. Now, that wasn't so bad was it??? Yeah, that's right, you liked it di'nt chew??? Now, I'm going to take a dump in your hot mouth Mr. Bossman. Here it comes…keep that mouth open or I'm going to slap you very hard and then kick you hard in your shins…

There's Nothing wrong with <u>**YOU**</u>. It's all a matter of perspective. Your Boss IS a hater who needs to drink Gaytorade or Kool Aid with tons of sugar in it! Have a wonderful day Bri Bri!

Most people are <u>**HATERS**</u> as they were raised in chaotic situations. They should be drinking **Haterade** to kill them.

My friend, Brion's boss called him Mini-Me the other day: I replied, "At least you look like somebody famous. You're really Maxi-Me, Maxi-Pad or Maxed out Mini-Me." Something like that. I told him I was related to 'Miss Piggy & Kermit the Frog' from The Muppets.

NAARP = National Association for the Advancement of Rainbow People. I'd rather join the NAARP vs NACCP: The National

If it wasn't for my wonderful twisted sense of humor I'd be in PRISON! Tell fag boss Ashley sez "hi, how are things going! She wishes you the best day evahhh!!!" Enjoy traveling with no diapers.

Sorry To Heart About Your Bad Luck: What bad luck? I didn't know I had any luck at all…

The Force is with Luke. The Farce is with me. Anybody know what a farce IS???

I just got a new job. I'm working @ Jordan's Meats here in Portland, Maine. I hang out in the bathroom and suck off all the hot guys when they take their breaks.

A meat packer is somebody who belongs to a **Meat Packers Union** or somebody like me who likes packing meat in hot cornholes and taking people to Poundtown.

JOIN! The Meat Packers Union: we play the game Cornhole. It's a FREE GROUP! NO MEMBERSHIP REQUIRED.

I told my friend, Chrissy Snow (Chris) that my meat is wrapped in a rubberband **AGAIN**! I told him I'm trying to choke him to death but all he does is spit at me. So rude he is. His name is Anaconda. Anybody want to see my Anaconda? I promise not to let him spit at you unless you want me to have him spit at you.

I've got a dead chicken between my legs. It's due to my age. What's a boy to do???

Constipated from sitting too much: that happens to the best of US!!!

I asked my friend, Chris, "How's your wife doing? Did she shit herself **<u>AGAIN</u>**!"

THE Cunt of The Month: that would be ME!!!

Congratulations, You're A Winner = Congratulations, you're a wiener lover. Who doesn't like putting big wieners in their mouth and licking them before eating them??? I surely do. Anybody want to see me put a big wiener in my mouth...you sir look like you would have a great time IF I put your wiener in my mouth

Somebody better piss up my ass very soon. I can't wait to feel it going in my hottt butt after the guy who pisses up my butt fucks the shit out of me and dumps his soup in me. Then he can felch it out.

SOUNDS LIKE FUN: riding a rollercoaster with a dildo up my ass. I'm going to have to pass on that idea as I know what's going to happen and it tain't pretty. **<u>NO THANKS</u>**!!!

Figure It Out = Finger It Out

I know of this woman whose name is Peggy and she's a Professional PCA who likes ripping her clients off and taking advantage of the time clock by not working all of her hours and she's definitely a denial queen as she won't ever admit to being a thief. She has a client who gets constipated regularly and she has to dig shit out of their ass. That's definitely a job for me. Then I can fling it at the client and say, "See what you made me do. See what you made me do."

Everybody has their healing identity besides feeling like Nuclear Waste

What's urine name honey? Mines is Lil Bo Peep or Little Beau Peep or Rainbow Childe

My names Diaper Pail Maverick. My step-father gave me a wigga name growing up: Big Red. My sister got the name of Half Pint and my half-brother got the name of Short Stop. Guess he liked baseball. I like water sports. That's the only Sport that I do like. I'm not that good at other Sports like baseball, basketball, etc.

Nigga = Wigga

Honey = Horny

Git 'er done with the drunk boy. He definitely wants it. I can taste it at the back of my throat.

Master Sir, Sir Master, how can I help you Master? What would you like me to do today???

My new boyfriend has the best suction than any man I've ever encountered: He's a cockpump and he really knows how to suck me dry. He never complains when I use him and when he breaks down I just send him back to the company that makes them and ask for a new one.

I'm getting blown right now: It's AWESOME!!! Wish You Were Here to join in!!! Have a beautiful lay! Yes, I'm using my cockpump to make my dick bigger. Those things really do work. Does anybody want me to demonstrate my cockpump next time I come to this Comedy Club? It can be arranged. Or, does anybody want to come to my place of have me come to their place to demonstrate how to use a cockpump?

Have A Beautiful Day = Have A Beautiful Lay

I'm a tall drink of mean, lean, rough 'n tough all over. I love myself no matter what. A bit nippy today but what else is new??? The love and happeniss brigade's here to see you through...

I'm getting **RAPED TODAY**! It's going to be a smokin' hot when it happens!!! Just made a new friend. His name's John and he knows another friend of mine I've known for 20++ years. He's addicted to Adderall. Go figure!

If a group of guys was going to rape me I'd tell them, "Make it Hurt So Good."

Don't make promises. I have the peppers. Stuff them up my ass so I'll cry like a baby.

Kneeling Benches are great. Speaking of kneeling benches what's up with a kneeling bus? Is that a bus that kneels and gives great blow jobs???

The only part of religion that I actually like: It won't be long before the end: when we die it's something to look forward to, not to fear in your heart of hearts. I look forward to dying. It's just a matter of time before it happens and I have a clear loving perspective towards dying when I do think about it. No sense in getting upset about death.

It's so much easier to see the past from a distance and forget about it by putting it in a Pandora's Box...make sure you lock the box with three locks. When the past comes calling, let it go to voicemail. You don't need it anymore. Just remember to remember the 'Good Times' you had when growing up when you lived as a child, etc. That's the best that you can do...**FORGET YOUR PAST**! It's like a ghost hanging around with you who won't leave you alone...**STOP!** arguing with your reality or with reality. You don't need that PAIN & SUFFERING as Hell IS Your Negative Thoughts that you still cling to that make you miserable. It's much easier to be at peace with your past than to think mean angry thoughts about what was done to you as a child. You survived that so this means that you are a **TROOPER**!!! Think about **THAT**!!!

Smile if you had it last night: Yes, I did get it last night. I touched my self. Why is it when I ask people to S M I L E if they had it last night they automatically think I said, "You got laid?" I just asked you to SMILE. I don't want to know about your personal sexual history.

I'd love to check into **The Hotel California** and never leave as I still have work to do before I actually do check out in this lifetime. That's why I'm **HERE NOW**! you can check out, but, you can never leave.

"We project our own reality on to other people" Not something you want to be doing. Sometimes, it's best to keep your mouth shut and live in the present moment. It really IS!!!

Think how much better you feel when you leave the meat **ALONE**! Give it a chance to breathe and air out! Why not just take off all of your clothes and **LIVE THE NUDIST LIFE** in your home???!!! Down with a Stinky Dinky, up with the meat thermometer. Just don't blow it right away: **THAT'S THE LESSON**. According to Ayurvedic Medicine one does not need to cum more than one time per week. That's four times per month. That's IT! However, I realize that I'm stepping on my lips. My good friend, Erik says, "Coming is a great way to release anger and rage issues." I concur.

"Later today honey pie: You can throw your **Happy Meal** at me anytime you like." What is a Happy Meal anyways??? Anybody want a Happy Meal right now? And, you get a toy with your Happy Meal.

No Problem Master Sir: it's been awhile since I took my meat out of the fridge! Not sure if it's any good. I've got to check the expiration date on my meat!!! It might be stale but still edible. It's delicious meat to eat anyways. I love it when people eat my meat and make me 'A Happy Camper'!!! It warms the cackles in my heart of hearts!!!

What About Us = "There is NO US!!!" I said to a good friend, Chris M.

Rubbers work when you need them unless they're bands of plastic. They don't last very long unless they're medical rubber bands that are used in surgery. I'm **THE RUBBERBAND MAN**!!!

It's very tasty: can't believe you haven't had it **YET**! Good Luck trying to get it!!! I'm living **THE INTENTIONAL LIFE**: Mindfulness and not rushed. You do the same. I love your outfit you're wearing. It reminds me of the one I had as a child when I lived in Germany. I was a little German Boy then from America.

What's red, white, huge and sits in the corner: Maverick Ashley Lenartson sitting in the corner masturbating his Moby Dick…

Does anybody know what a meat thermometer is??? I've never held one in my hands. Don't leave the meat in the fridge for too long as it's going to get soft and raunchy. You know what happens when you leave the meat in the fridge for too long…or, up somebody's ass…it just falls out. Then you have to put it back in the fridge.

I bought a pocket pussy and a pocket asshole to keep me happy at The Treasure Chest the other day. It's the best investment that I've ever made in my life…

I want my Happy Meal, I want my Happy Meal [say it like a petulant little child]

A Course in Miracles: It's a miracle when I get out of bed before the sun starts going down on me.

I like going to Porn Palaces and licking the floors after a hot guy leaves the booth. It gets me off…

Cops = PIGS

COCKCUCKERS = Copsuckers or ME. Those cocksuckers came to my apartment **AGAIN**! **WTF**! Those copsuckers…don't they have anything else better to do…

Washington Gardens = Shithole Gardens

Buddha has sex. Just because we think he's nasty with that fat stomach of his or hers doesn't mean that being slothy doesn't work for him: this only means that he's full from overeating but he has a smile on his face like a pig does as he's satisfied and happy that he ate a really good meal. It doesn't mean that Buddha doesn't like **S-E-X**…it's really a matter of perspective with being Buddha…fat Buddha boy!!!

It doesn't matter if you are clean or not: your dicks nasty from not showering regularly. Some guys are just like that!!! That's why I'm thinking whipped cream

or honey: makes a nasty dick taste so much better. One can overlook that stink and not throw up when they are busy trying to suck a nasty dick.
Personally, I don't know if I want to lick your asshole as it's even nastier than your stinky dinky…don't take this personally. It's not meant to be an attack on your beautiful kind soul…

I think that if you have a prefrontal lobotomy you are going to end up becoming a different person. Personally I'd rather have my whole brain removed so that I cannot think anymore as hell is my thoughts. I think that you're a little boy who needs to love himself: I'd love to fuck a guy like that!!! But, not a woah!man…if you know what I mean…

I'd love to see a man with no nuts. What's that going to accomplish honey??? You saw a man with NO NUTS. You can still be castrated. You're going to have to ask your new doctor in Lewiston, Maine to do it for you! He's going to ask you why you want to be castrated and you can tell him why. Of course, you're going to have to pay out of pocket expenses to be castrated as it isn't something that is done to an Adult unless there is a medical problem and even then one must think carefully why the want their nuts chopped off. It's a very serious thing to think about and contemplate but I truly understand that being a dancer might be a reason to have your nuts chopped off…Just remember that when you have your nuts medically removed that you are going to regret it and think about that fact that you cannot produce hormones anymore so why even consider that move??? The reason you are fuct up emotionally is because you agreed to have a vasectomy when you were in your teens. And, of course you're going to feel like a transsexual as you're going to still have a penis but you will be nutless…you're basically a little girl running around out there with **NO NUTS**! How insane is **THAT**!!!??? **THINK ABOUT IT**…just think about it very carefully before you go down that route…personally, I'd rather be a woman but I don't have 60,000.00dollarslying around in a bank account that I can spend to have myself turned into a woman and the whole thought about doing that to me is **NUTS, JUST PLAIN NUTS**! I like being a man and having a dick, nuts and an asshole: I own a mangina. That's what I own. I'm not technically a woah!man but I do have a **MANGINA**! that I let guys use for the pleasure as it gives me pleasure to make a man happy when he fucks the shit out of me. The Mangina Monologues is a book I need to write NEXT…

I once had sex with a guy who surgically had his nuts removed for some reason. Next time I see him I'm going to ask him why his nuts were removed. He may not answer the question...

When you want your nuts removed just ask the Taliban to do it. They're a very Sadistic Barbaric Race of People. I never want to meet them. One cannot just assume that just because one is gay, an Emo, a Christian, a Catholic, etc. that their head needs to be chopped off...it's an insane in the membrain way to live...it really IS...**NO THANKS**!!!

I have a friend by the name of Brion who's Aunt raised him as a girl **PRIVATELY**. Now, he's obsessed about being a girl and not wanting to be one...I wonder why...

The reason I write books and pop songs is because I'm a sensitive man and that kind of stuff helps me to heal **ME**...especially when I have a hair across my crack...one that is ingrown and causing me pain that needs to be pulled out with tweezers or two strong hands...

I was never really bullied in high school however, my twin-sister, Rosy, was looking out for me when I got to high school as she knew better what boys and girls of a young age are like: she told people not to bully me. It apparently worked. But, there was this one boy by the name of Richard Daigle who couldn't keep his mouth shut. So, he'd bully me with his mouth while standing in the lunch line waiting for lunch and I went up to him one day because I got sick of hearing him mock me in public by mouthing out my name **ASHLEY** in a high pitched voice and I walked out of the line and up to him and stood up to the bully and said not a word. Then I went back to my place in line and he didn't bully much anymore except for an occasional bullying with his big mouth. He just had to have the last word as he never learned no better. That's the way of most of the human race. It really IS...Bullys SUCK. They need to be put in their place. That's the only way they are ever going to learn to keep their mouths shut...it really does work...the only problem is that they are itching for a fight as that's what they really want...

I'm pumping my dick right now as you read these words: the best thing I ever bought is a cockpump to make my dick bigger than it really is...my cockpump is now my best friend in the world.

See you later = smell you later, much later…

When I have to get rid of junk in my apartment I make sure that I take off all of my clothes to work on that issue alone…it's a lot of fun to sort through papers in the middle of the night in the nude for 15 minutes a day until I can take it no more…

Have fun sucking. I do. I suck at being a human being but that is ok with me. I'm perfectly fine with that…

I love giving hot head to guys who love a great BJ from an experienced guy who knows what he is doing…

What would my life be like if I had a pussy? I'd probably have a verbally and physically abusive boyfriend who wants to take me anytime he likes. **NO THANKS**!!!

Nobody wants to be miserable like you are…or do they??? There is no such thing as happiness without having to be miserable so one may as well be miserable…

If I had a boyfriend, I'd cheat on him all the time as a realationship with a male or female hasn't worked out for me in this lifetime so I'm not going to worry about something that hasn't happened yet. No time for THAT!!!

I told my friend, Brion, "You're nothing more than a cum dumpster to me who reminds me of me…My Big Fat Bitch!!! I get to abuse you as much as that gets me off…

I also told Brion to get another boyfriend who does what he likes him to do. Sounds like the Co-Worker relationship thing to me. Not a healthy way to have a boyfriend relationship. No Thanks!

I also told him, "You're my big fat bitch and I love hating on YOU because you get off on that way of life and living. You're a filthy fat pig whore who has boundary issues. So what!!! I like when you **SHUT UP & DO AS I SAY, NOT AS YOU WISH!** You're my "Slave Bitch", that's what you are to me…

I also told him, "You'd be much happier in **PRISON**: then you'd think about sex, food and shitting everyday of your incarceration."

"The guy likes Ron because he looks like a stud. You and I both need to lose weight, period. We're both fat disgusting pig troll bulls. However, I don't mind that rain. It's to be expected because April Showers…

When are you free to suck my big smelly dick??? I should wait a cuppa days to give you my load.

"Did you shit your diaper on purpose just to get attention **<u>AGAIN</u>**??? Or, it just happened because the doctor paralyzed your bladder with botox **AGAIN**??? I'd rather have your problems than have prostate issues at my age but my prostate hasn't been acting up sooo…

I've come to the conclusion that my friend, Brion J., is an Adult Baby and that he likes being treated as such as he has dissociation disorder due to his schizophrenia and his disturbed childhood. I'm glad that I'm not him and that I'm a **FREE MAN**…

I will not jerk off for a few days. Then you can go to town on my Uncut Oscar Meyer Wiener…

I told my friend, Brion J, "You should be as miserable as possible. That way you will end up being happy. Be a Pessimist while you are at it! You would do such good at it!"

"If you want the load, wait 'til Friday."

Funny Comedy for Depressed People

I know why my good friend, Joseph C., doesn't want to get laid: paranoia about Social Diseases and Older Age…

My friend Brion is the crazy brother that I never had while growing up all around the world as my step-father was in the military. My step-father was definitely Illuminati but he wasn't none too bright…he was a follower, not a leader. I'm a swallower, not a fearless leader. The Illuminati are not 'People of The Light,' most of them are Control Freaks bent on destroying the planet and killing as many people as possible. Why go to the gas chambers when they can bring the gas chambers to us???

I'm working…hardly working

Become an Adult Baby: that way your needs get taken care of in a round-a-bout way. You love sucking your thumb. That tells me you have unmet needs witch is ok by me. We all do.

I want to take a big smelly dump all over you then smear it around

Has anyone here ever butt dialed somebody with their cell smartphone? I sure have. "Who is this…who is this." [slurping sucking noises heard in the background]

I'm disgusted with your behavior = I'm dicksgusted with your behavior

I have ODD = Oppositional Dick Sucking Disorder as I only do it for the money not Oppositional Defiance Disorder as some people have told me

I'm not slurprised that I act the way that I do

Just think about how different you'd be if you got the love you wanted as a child: you'd **_STOP!_** throwing tantrums when around me…

Normal people have no problem with being bitches…

Wouldn't want to be ya, ya, ya, ya, ya…NO WAY HOSE!

Stick it up yer ass, I insist!!!

I seriously doubt that you bought whipped cream or honey, honey. Send me a pix of it. Anybody who takes showers once a month is a dirty fuckpig and a monster. What's your monster name???   I'm 'Little Beau Peep' and I'm wild in the streets of Portland, Maine. I'm also wild between the sheets of my bed…

I love wearing diapers up the streets of Portland, Maine just to make people laugh.

My specialty: making people laugh their butts off. It gets me off in a comedic way. Wouldn't it be something IF I could come from laughing or just making people laugh. Then I'd want to do it all the time.

If you want to be HAPPY you have to go thru HELL to get it. I suggest that a person be miserable as it's much easier to become happy from being miserable, not the other way around. Much easier to manage when one thinks about it.

I'm a **Krazy Beatch Master**. That's what **I YAM**!!! My middle names **FUN FUN FUN**…

On you or me??? You can only have one thing shaved as your time is at a **PREMIUM** with me dear!!!

If I want to get laid I have to put on women's clothes and makeup and speak as a woman…

I told my friend, Brion, "You tell me what you want me to do with you then I will do it." Yeah Right: I get to do whatever I want with any slave that I own as when they don't listen they get whipped by a belt, etc.

I love wiping my manhole: you know what they say: a clean hole is much better to lick than a shitty hole unless of course you like licking shit encrusted manholes…

Those who object to anything shall be made fun of or ridiculed severely…

SCREAM GARDENS: a place where you go to get your ya yas out or a theme park where you ride water rides or the rollercoasters

I'm Committed to Living My Life = I'm Cummitted to Living My Adult Life

The only sadistic object I need to shut my friend, Brion, up with is a ball gag made out of rubber, a piece of shitty underwear, dirty socks, etc. The more he objects the deeper into his mouth I shove these kinds of things…

I became a **fag** because I was good at being gay…it suits me just fine…

In the land of Dairy Queen, we treat you right = In the land of carpet munchers we treat you right…

My Favorite Subject: ME & my name: SHITHEAD

MANA: life giving juice down my throat

Drive me crazy all you want: I won't respond, unless of course, you start 'Tickle Fest' with me. Then I'm going to laugh my ass off…

With a longing in my feart of fearts

Come Together: who doesn't like coming together in more ways than one???

Other names for cum: baby batter, cool whip, whipped cream, a cigarette filter doused with nail polish remover, buttahh, white frosting, and olive oil

Everybody has their price. I charge by the inch.

NOBODYS PERFECT = However, I'm PERFECT AS I AM

My girlfriend and I are celebrating the three year anniversary of the day we met: HA HA HA HA HA HA HA!! Go Ahead: Have a great laugh about that one…

I love me: ha ha ha ha ha ha ha ahhhhhhhhhhhhh…said Chuckles the Clown

The only reason I'm queer is because my mother looked like a man and my step-father fucked me when I was a child. I'm ok with that…

Some people need to be abused just to reinforce the notion of **FREEDOM**. If more people allow this to happen then they are going to get wise very quickly to what it means to be **FREE**!!!

Foto Hut = Foto Slut

"Since you are my slave you have to submit or else you get punished severely with the belt, the ruler or the whip! You need a sore ass and more!!! I'm Your Man!!! You need **TORTURE** my friend…that's what you really need to shut your hellish mind up! Then when you think about what you went through you are going to feel much better…

Welts from the leeches: HA! HA!

I'm going to shave you the next time you come over. When you persist I'm going to have to _ _ _ _ your _ _ _ _ _ and the more you resist the worse it's going to get!!!

I just damaged my arms in a car accident: come over to wipe my ass!!! Both arms are disabled and my name is Mo and I'm definitely a HO!!! HO HO HO HO HO…I charge 200 a session…I look like an escaped Carnival/Circus Act!

There is nothing wrong with a male being and acting like a female in Society: You persist w/o your estrogen and progesterone. You'd be much worse off so **STOP!** complaining. You sure that you are not a broken record player. You know there are people with worse problems out there that they are never going to overcome. Are you one of these people??? Me thinks soooooo…..

What's your cars' name: **CHRISSY**??? My cars name is **THE BOMBER**. I got pulled over the other day by the Feds as I spray painted the words on the side of my car. Imagine the feeling when they ripped my car a new asshole. Now, my car is a shit car…I could care less…

Whipped Cream & Cherries. You already have the nuts to prove it! In more ways than one…

Who's got the biggest balls of them all??? AC/DC

Go ahead, make your self feel like shit when you wake up in the morning. You will snap out of it very quickly. It's called **REVERSE PSYCHOLOGY** or **REVERSE SUCKOLOGY**!

Mike Hawk smells like fermunga. I love the smell of fermunga. I love getting it on my fingers: I smell it then lick it off. It's a **SPECIAL ORDER CHEESE** that's very, very, very, very, very rare on account of the fact that it's an **ENDGANGERED CHEESE**! I can't get enough of it...

FABULOUS = FABULASS

They came and they went like a cheesy fart in the wind

The only way I can lick a nasty cheesy dick or ass that smells rotten is with whipped cream, honey or anything sweet like strawberries, etc.

Winner = Wienner

Little Beau Peep = Little Blo Peep

The sheep will come back on their own when it begins to get dark outside: they usually do unless they do get lost. Then somebody is going to find them and bring them back to you.

The Sun went down on me = Your son went down on me. We're dating now. It's just a sexual thing. It's not a realationship. He's on the rebound since his girlfriend left him.

I gotta take a big phat dump in the turlit. Later Dude, much latahhhhhhhhhhhhhhhhhhhhhhhhhh!!!!!!!!!!!!!!

My place smells fragrant now: I just took a dump in the toilet and flushed it down the drain...

I'm a Sad Camper: A SAD SACK

I wear Pampers diapers as I'm Socially Incontinent in more ways than one

BAM! BAM! BAM! says Pebbles!!!

MY BAD, MY BAD: what the fuck did you do NOW???!!! Who the fuck invented that saying? My Bad…

So sorry Charlie = So Solly Cholly

You don't play with your rooster enough. I have to go **SLOWLY** with **YOU**…I'm a **PRO COMEDIAN** compared to **YOU**…I need a cock cage to prevent me from masturbating and cumming all the time…I do it once per day. The most I've ever jerked off in one day is 5 times. **YES, I CAME** each time…I've heard of a guy who comes without touching himself and another guy who is able to pump out a load of hot cum 11 times in a row. Must be a multiple cummer. Women are so <u>**LUCKY**</u> because they are able to come 100++ times in one sitting…I wish I was a woman. No wonder they get depressed and sullen when they're boyfriend cums and then rolls over and goes to sleep. Women are a much different animal than a man ever will be…

Daddy says, "You will do as you are told." Go buy a cucumber, a carrot or a squash and shove it up your ass for practice. Daddy also says, "Ask Mo if she wants you to wipe her ass."

If Buddha is so wise why is he so fucking fat??? Why does he slap you when you ask him the meaning of life??? Because he's a **SLOTH** and he contemplates everything. He's definitely got **ANGER ISSUES** and that's why he calls himself **BUDDHA**. He's trying to reach Spiritual & Emotional Enlightenment with his issues/thoughts that go running through his head all day long…

Waiting develops the mind to fruition: it's called being **PATIENT**. The more you have to rush through your life to get things done the more you are not practicing **MINDFULNESS**. The two go hand in hand. **MINDLESSNESS** is not the way to go when rushing through your life at full speed.

I'm sure he does: He just doesn't tell anybody about it as that's his little secret. Everybody has **SECRET** and skeletons in their closet. I have a belly so I may as well start acting like **BUDDHA** = **BUD HA**!

MOTOR MOUTH = little children who don't stop talking or ME as a comedian

You are so horny because you have been pumping that cock of yours **AGAIN**! haven't you??? The pumping action causes pressure on your whole groin area and actually helps your prostate produce more sperm! It's great to do at any age. Besides, you're going to end up with a plump juicy Oscar Meyer Wiener and people who look at it are going to be **AMAZED** at the size and girth of your wiener…
It's not necessarily going to get longer, it's going to get fatter.

My friend, Chris, told me he needs another rubber band: I told him to ask the mail delivery guy for one. He's got plenty of them kicking around in his bag of mail.

I can edge by leaving mike hawk alone!

Like I keep saying, I have a brain. I'm one of the fartest people here at Troll Island. However, I'm not that smelly unless I fart and it comes out wet. That's cobra Mary's problem with her stooge boyfriend, Danny!!! Ha ha ha ha ha ha ha………….

Is there a UNION for puppets and marionettes??? What was life like before toilet paper, electricity, washing machines and outhouses: **very stinky**!!!

How many lesbians do you need to change a lightbulb? Silly, everybody knows that most lesbians don't know how to change lightbulbs as they remind them of inflated penises with bulbous heads on them.

You get drunk and end up sucking 9 maybe 10 dicks in one night. And you say, "I'm not gay." OK.

APPRECIATION for the male figure…or, the female figure…

CONSULTANT: 207-809-9461 CALL ME! NO PROBLEM TOO BIG!!! I like Big Things...

There's a Turd Stooge in there: turd eye of Mary & Daddy: they're joined at the hips and the lips!!!

As long as you put fermunga cheese in it, I'll eat it!!!

A sense of humor is required to work with **ME**!!!

That's **HOW WE ROLL**!!!

Jelly Roll

My favorite desert: TWINKIES

You are never **ALONE** thanks to your thoughts...your thoughts are **HELL** most of the time...there is really no hell to speak of, or heaven for that matter in your mind. Heaven is **INSIDE OF YOU**!!!

In order to work with somebody who is not your skin color you have to overlook the other persons skin color...that's what you have to do...you also have to listen very well and not respond to anything negative that the person says...

Ink Masters Angels: Kelly Dody w/ her green hair. What's up with the green hair? Is she trying to tell us that she is Irish???!!!

Confucious say: Itchy bum means me take bath now. No, now you have smelly finger!

Sticky Mucky Spunk Texters

Trailer Jokes for people who consider themselves Trailerpark Trash

Roland N. Dough

Dixie Chicks = Chixie Dicks

Gimmer your black babies: I want to swallow them all

I want to get fucked behind a dumpster @ The Maine Mall or in the woods near Little Beau Peeps home or perhaps, underneath a bridge nearby.

Have to put an ad on fakeslist: Need your help: Looking for a Surrogate Daddy. That'll make people go **WTF!** Butt, I'm going to get replies for sure but the ad will get **BANNED by IDIOTS** who think they know better but they will never learn better…they will never learn no better because they don't know when to mind their own fucking business…they're basically **ASSHOLES**.

You make me want to throw up = I said that to my girlfriend once and she slapped me **HARD!**

Can't stop, won't stop laughing my butt off…I laugh at least 50++ times per day. It keeps me HAPPY because of those endorphins that get released from the laughter.

Bob wants to have sex with the two of us. Yes, I'm a krazy kraka. That's what I am. I don't have a problem with being **THAT**!!!

Book Titles: **Trading Insults/Jokes 101: Terrible Jokes you can use on your unsuspecting enemies**…

The Complete Jokeology Book Mike Hunt: A to Z – Ridiculousness Jokes for Ridiculous People

White Christmas = Wide Christmas or somebody coming in your mouth, ass or vagina…

My Life Does Not Revolve Around Your Weekend

Cross Dressing Thief Leaves One Breast Behind…what happened to the other breast? Did it get left in front???

Jaywalker allegedly moons motorists after ticket…anyone want to see the full moon tonight or an eclipse of my butt tonight???

THE Society For Evil Christians

I bet your favorite flavor of ice cream is Moose Tracks

TOP STRESS REDUCERS by Donald Foster Adapted by Ashley P Braine Lennartsson **(The 12 Step Program)**

1. Drink beer
2. Smoke Cigarettes
3. Be **BITCHY**
4. Think of nasty things to do to people
5. Stick **PINS** in your **VooDoo Dolls**: come up with images of people you **HATE**
6. Litter on your neighbor's lawn(s)
7. Ignore everyone, except important calls
8. Grunt unintelligibility when spoken to
9. Think of at least **3 Negative Thoughts** (or more in some cases) per day
10. **Don't feed your boa constrictor**: he may strangle someone or eat a pet
11. Put tin cans in the trash to annoy Conservative minded friends
12. Talk dirty to your plants

Michael Jackson

If it's before 8, it's too late

Michael Jackson's favorite food: chicken. After all, he was black. I'm white so my favorite meat to eat was Michael Jackson.

The Tell All Book he was writing before he passed??? Confessions of a Chicken Queen, Part I

Getting stopped by a cop in a "**NO SPEEDING ZONE**" for students – My excuse – I ate a pound of sugar cookies. He let me go.

Remember that when you have to go to court for a **Traffic Ticket** to get out of it all you have to do is keep asking for a continuance of the case. Eventually it will be dropped.

Religious people are so self-righteous. I'll never forget the 1st time Jan & I were driving along The 'Sea of Gallile' and Jesus pulled up behind **US**!!! And, I'll never forget as Jan woke up and I began sucking on my cock while Jesus watched us going at it and then he asked us to join in. Jan said, "It's about time that you had some relief."

Look in the mirror and really examine what you look like and judge every pore of your skin. Then laugh about it. It's a big joke to look in the mirror and to laugh at your self and then go, "I guess I'm going to have to get some retinol with Vit. A, Caritol and Vit. C to put on my face." Or, you could just put some sperm or egg white on your face and wait for it to create a really tight mask and then wash it off later. Or, you could just spray your self with Olive Oil or Cactus Juice to help your skin become tighter and smoother so that you look much younger than you really are...

Friends = friends only want you for three reasons: **1.** To talk to you about their problem **2.** To fuck you for money **3.** To borrow money **4.** To borrow something that they forget to return and refuse to return like the money. After all, the money is considered a '**LOVE GIFT**'.

Friends with babies = you can just forget about taking care of their kids unless you and your family do things together.

Straight vs Faggot = you have to look beyond a person's sexuality in order to get to know them. Not all straight guys want their dick sucked by a woman as most women don't like to swallow loads as they think it's very nasty. That's the real reason that a guy goes to another guy for hot sex. Just don't mention the word, "**GAY**" with him because most straight guys who get their dick sucked by another guy would tell you that they are **NOT GAY**!!! "It's not true, it's not true, I'm not a homosexual. I'm not a homosexual." – Robert I

Funny situations = the phone rings when you are on the toilet and you forgot to bring your cell phone in the loo with you...

Is **THAT** why you are acting like a 2 year old??? Because you can't get your way **TODAY**??? Time to throw a temper tantrum…

DOUBLE ENTENDRE: Penis/Asshole/Dick, Doctor, B.M. 7:00 pm, while we're still in bed

What's up with the roommates who leave piss filled soda bottles behind? What about the roommate who fell asleep half naked with his penis in his hand with porn playing on the computer???

Why is cutting the cheese such a bad thing??? Why is that when a woman does it most of the time she won't admit it??? What's up with THAT??? Men are so different from women. They love talking about their farts. They love sniffing their own farts. Most women won't do that??? As a matter of fact all men really ever do all day longer is think about their dick and their asshole. Women think about what they can get out of a man, how they can make fun of him and how they can corner him on something he said two months ago. That's why I'm **GAY**!!!

On being a cat = most of them are just plain finicky. Watch out when you transmit negative energy to a cat and then try to pet it. You might get bitten. Send them '**Positive Energy**' as they transmit all those vibrations somewhere in the Universe. If I knew where I'd tell you.

Martha Stewart "**It's a Good Thing. A Good Thing.**"

Potty Mouth Inc.

The Cookies Cutter Comic: He likes making cookies and feeding them to his audience.

Ask someone for a beer before your do your set on stage and then spend the whole time drinking the beer and speaking to your audience. The beer is going to relax you and make you forget your whole act unless of course, you have it all memorized upstairs in that funny brain of yours.

Herpes = how many people have herpes and got it from their other half???

I've got a really big fish story to tell you

Ashley Mouse. I'm related to Minnie & Mickey Mouse

You look like shit: 'tis better to feel like shit than to look like shit

Running personals in the Casco Bay Weekly. Why bother. It usually doesn't work out.

What's up with alcoholic slumlords??? That's the question that you have to ask before you move in. You must ask questions like, "Who's your worst tenant?" "Why did you become a slumlord in the 1st place?" "How many years have you been in business?" "Do you like what you are doing with your life?" "Got any great tenant stories?"

Part time animals: animals were put here to make man feel greater love as they are usually unconditional and they end up becoming like their owners when owned.

Part time smokers: what's up with people who smoke part-time???

Welcome to Masturbationland

Part Time Lesbians: Rug Burners who like the other sex

On smoking pot: Is there such a thing as a pothead???

The Pause That Refreshes: C O M E D Y

Stamp out comedy like you make sugar cookies with a cookie cutter and become a Cookie Cutter Comic at times comedy is fast, furious and fun fun fun...

Mike Hunt, please come to the office. Mike Hunt...

Cigarettes are for people who can't slow down with their thoughts

A New Habit: has anyone ever formed a new habit that isn't registered yet with the **American Medical Association**??? Anybody??? Not the usual habits to pass the time away like sex, drinking and smoking pot. It's got to be something that is 'Out of This World' and it makes you happy and people don't necessarily know that you are doing it…like walking around with a butt plug up your ass or ???

Billy Fudge Packer

Sally Fudge Packer

Billy Fudge Packee

Sally Fudge Packee

Silly Fudge Packer: fudge is for children and adults she told me one day

FUDGE PACKERS 'R US!!! There's nothing wrong with packing fudge. H.F. Fudgepacker would agree with me. He works for the Keebler Fudge Packing Company and makes cookies. He likes packing the fudge. Just don't get any on me…

I'm Not Playing with a Full Deck of Cards: I lost the Ace, the Queen of Spades & the Joker

My Elevator Doesn't Go All The Way To The Top

Lorena Bobbitt = whatever happened to her and does anybody want to get Bobbittized???

Crack = anybody got any crack??? Well, if I can't get any crack I'll settle for red smelly crack to lick.

Banana Split = Boneana Split

Little Miss Muffet = what did she really sit on??? A big phat _ _ _ _ . And, did it make her scream out in pain because it was too big like that spider???

Mary Had A Little Lamb: Mary had a baby because she couldn't keep her legs shut!!!

Door Handles = you can actually sit on a door handle, you know, the one with the knob on it that is round and big and it's going to go up your wahzoo, your snatch, or your mouth.

Car Sex = anybody ever had car sex???

Endorphins = they keep you happy
Ass Clips = What are ass clips??? I mean forceps…

Rob Banks = he's a very good friend of mine. He likes to…

Welcome to Mental Retardation Land (No Offense Taken): everybody's mentally retarded to some degree or other as there are things that simply should not be attempted by anybody unless that is their DREAM!!!

Mavericks' Fuck 'N Suck, how may I help you?

Koala Bear = that's the name of my girlfriend. I know, I know. She looks like a Koala Bear and she loves bearback sex.

Baby Changing Station: something that I avoid as I don't have any babies

1-800-4-A-POTTY

1-800-4-BLOW

Bo Great

Blow Job = anybody like sucking on big things tonight?

Kitty Kats = anybody like scarring kitty kats?

Oprah Winfrey = HARPO Productions = for a while I thought Oprah was going to turn into a whale. Then she was in the media **_AGAIN_** running to lose that weight. You know when you have a lot of money you can afford to eat where you like and what you like and that's what makes you get FATTER.

Roseanne Barre = LOUD MOUTH

Tom Arnold = Reminds me of a pig

Sylvester the Cat: he's always getting into trouble w/ grandma catching him trying to eat Tweedy Bird

Tweedy Bird: he's such a big yellow bird with a big yellow head. What's up with that???

THE Portland Police Department: the reason they have such a tough job to do is because they're having to deal with the same situations over and over and over AGAIN!

Jerk Meat = what exactly **IS** Jerk Meat? Beef Jerky? Something else. Anybody want to reach down into my backpack and give me my beef jerky? How about my pants? I've got excellent jerk meat down there for anybody who loves making me **HARD**!

What's up with Bitchy Swans = did you know that a bitchy swan can actually kill a human being. They're really nasty birds when they get pissed off at you.

The Young & The Restless = The Young & The Restless, The Young, The Old, Middle Aged & **THE** Restless

Hey You = Who ME???

Why are paranoid schizophrenics so paranoid? I have a friend of mine by the name of Peggy W. who keeps saying, "Who me?"

Country Twang

Rap Beat

Marylin Monroe

Hillary Clinton = Killary Clinton

Sea Dogs = what exactly is a Sea Dog: a Sea Dog or somebody from the Portland, Maine Sea Dogs baseball team?

I walkd up 2u it wz th othr nite @th eastern prom u hd on white tites thn i askd 2suk ur ck thru ur pantz u said gime twenty thn im going 2tak al my cloths off thn we kan boff i said r u crazy rite out here in th open u said hey im not queer u btr gt dat strait nowcumonovrher n sukmybait i said r u klean u said yesaw mastrbates get ovr her 2finis me off or il let tht fat queah who liks lyk santa klaus gt th job dun as i no hes hungry 4my hotcum i said no problm sir wud u rathr stik it in mebum its bn a whil sinc i let anybdy cum u said oh litl blo peep u r so wild n free oh litl bo peep why dnt u fk me hard oh litl bo peep lets not get married i said thts a deal i hav 1 wife but i bet she wnt blow me as wel as u wil cum on ovr here & do wht u wil kant wait

Biff Barnaby = one of my porn names or a sleuth

Life Is Fun when you are on alcohol, marijuana, pills or food

Prozac = the last time I stole a friends medication I wanted to kill people for two days after taking it
Lithium is made for batteries. Why would you want to put that into a person?

Haldol = anybody ever heard of the Haldol shuffle???

Heroin = That's the only drug that can motivate me to do anything

I need downers to calm me down, not uppers to calm me up

I hired a new maid who's completely stupid and only listens to my slumlord, Donald. All she ever says is,
"Yessa Masta, Yes sa."

Needs: friendlier, less fucked up tenants

A warmer client to live in: that's what I could use

More money: who doesn't like having more money in their life? As in Mo Money!

A newer house to live in. I just love that fresh house smell like when I buy a new truck with Corinthian Leather

Less Ignorant Maine Residents

People who actually pay attention and who don't say **"YES"** just to say 'YES'. I'm now a **NO MAN**. I like saying **NO** to addicts. I don't need any more addicts in my life.

COMEDY – MAKING TRACKS

Walk on stage: crooked gait. I bet you thought I was suffering from some malady didn't you? I just wanted to observe how gullible some of your people are

Crazy people = The Crazy Lady. Whatever happened to the crazy lady down the road? She finally died.

Snack Ramen Noodles = MSG is like a drug as it makes you high and gives you hives and a headache. What's up with that?

Squirrel Talk = I have a friend by the name of Loran Gann who likes to speak in squirrel talk

Manic Depression/Bi-Polar = I have a mental health issue. I don't see it as a barrier to living my life. I'm actually a Bi Polar Bear who lives in Portland, Maine. I like having sex with other bi-polar bears

Schizophrenic people are very smart people. You have to watch out for them as they will best you most of the time.

Drink 6-8 cups of really finds Brazilian **Coffee** before going to bed. Find out what happens besides not being able to sleep. You are going to turn into a Psychic and pick up the negative energy that people throw out at each other.

Michael Jackson = I really don't know what the hell happened to him. He definitely turned into a freak

Drinking – If I'm going to be drinking alcohol-uh-I usually don't drink-well then, I like to slam it down very quickly. Like the time I celebrated with employees where I used to work: Boone's Restaurant on Commercial Street. Alcohol makes me do things I usually don't do. Feeling up a female, bending over and feeling like Rover, driving my bicycle home drunk weaving from right to left on the road being careful not to cross the yellow line on Congress Street. What's up with THAT???

Going to a bar and drinking Bud Light Beers – It's alright but since I bought pitchers of it and had not drink beer for a while, I sucked the beer straight from the pitcher all in a matter of 1 ½ hours and proceeded to leave the bar feeling very good about myself. I like that fact that I don't get nasty when I drink beer in public. I turn into a happy drunk. I'm very lucky there.

Miller Light – its piss beer. It may have a golden look and flavor but the best part about drinking any beer is the head the beer gives me. I never thought it was possible to get head from beer but it sure is possible: **foam**. Want more foam in your beer: pour table salt in your beer. Mix the beer with your spoon or chopstick and all that head magically appears. Next time you need a little bit of head, drink some beer. The beer takes the place of the woman. Miller Light doesn't smell like piss, but the color and the taste sure do remind me of piss. Of course, if you like drinking piss well then you are all set. That's your kind of beer, not mine. Of course, if you happen to be **GAY** and like drinking piss, nah—forget I said that. I don't want to insult half of my audience tonight.

Just because a straight man likes to suck cock and take it up the ass doesn't mean that he is **GAY**. It just means that he's a **COCKSUCKER** & he has a mangina between his legs. Just don't ask him if he is **GAY**!

ASS SNIFFER

Future Jokes: what are jokes from the future: IMPROVISATION!

I told my mom to have a conversation with her relatives, her mother, father and brother. What's up with that??? They're all dead…

The Tobin Bridge – who doesn't like being in the middle of a bridge during Rush Hour

Answering Machine Messages: weird calls in the middle of the night or at any other time of the day. What's up with that???

Stupid Human Tricks. How many times can you say, "Hi," in one day and someone says, "Not!" or nothing. They don't even smile at you. Baby, same shit, different day. Wouldn't it be nice if someone said, "I'm Ecstatic." That would be nice.

Jokes For Gay People

Cream of Sperm Soup from Campbells

The Sperm Burgler from McBungholes Restaurant

The Sperm Burper Highway by I.M. Harder

Sperm Drop Cookies

Sperm Drop Candy

I'm the middle child. No wonder I need attention all the time. I'm the stupid one according to my parents but I'm simply not buying that anymore. Thank God I'm not being verbally and physically abused anymore. I'm a **FREE MAN**!!!

Thank God Daddy Didn't Pull Out

My Mamas Better Than Your Mama

Off Like A Prom dress

Excellent = Egg sell ent

Surprised = Slurprised

Business = Bizznass

What's Up!!!

What's up with raising a boy as a girl? Or, a girl as a boy???

Soft, Easy & Refreshing: my bf or gf

Forgive Your Self: that's the only person you can forgive

Women are only good for sucking the money out of my bank account, having children and throwing me in jail because anybody with a brain knows that women have all the rights in society

My favorite movie of all time is HOMO ALONE

I'm related to deep throat...he's my brother...

You have to be your own best friend: best friends are very hard to keep

I already got off as I'm not waiting for Mr. Right to show up as he's usually Mr. Wrong

Ronald Morris
Was in an auto accident but ok thanks for asking
Ashley Lenartson
you can use Ben Gay on it and he'll make you feel better...ha ha ha ha ha ha...I know, I know...I just made a joke

lots of loads, lots and lots and lots of white creamy dreamy loads of icing on the cake

Big Wood is the name of my new rock band or big woody

William Davis

Yum buddy, wanna give me some…

Maverick Ashley Lenartson

I'll bake a cake and put jizz in the icing for you.

William Davis

Down with the batter, I got the recipe

Maverick Ashley Lenartson

I know what the recipe requires

William Davis

How long to bake

Maverick Ashley Lenartson

I'll cum over to your house, whip out my dick, you start sucking me off: no muss, no fuss: it'll take as long as you like for the white icing to come out…you'll know when I'm done and your mouth is full of white icing…will that make you happier??? I sure hope so…

William Davis

I'll clean the house first, then I'll blow you

Maverick Ashley Lenartson

Don't bother cleaning the house: I've experienced worse trauma in my lifetime: not a big deal if your house is messy. You can clean it up after I leave.

William Davis

Oh wait, the cake

Maverick Ashley Lenartson

The cake has green icing and it's sitting in MacArthur Park

William Davis

Candy, raining in the dark, lol, you're a lot of fun

Maverick Ashley Lenartson

I know, I know…I'm a Cumedian…

William Davis

Yum hun. Lick it up!

Maverick Ashley Lenartson

That's it get all the green icing down your throat and tell me to bake another cake with green icing in MacArthur Park

William Davis

We could play well together
You'll say something & I'll twist it ever so

Maverick Ashley Lenartson

Some people say I have a "sick mind" but I don't pay no heed to them: they just don't understand the mind of a comic…I go from one topic to the next topic…I'm not an actor, I'm a seductive actress

William Davis

I'm a single sick fucka. It's all in my head

Maverick Ashley Lenartson

you mean mutha fucka...that's right, I had sex w/ my whole family - The Aristocrats

William Davis

And have a heart of gold and I'll still fucka you!
Mousecowits

Maverick Ashley Lenartson

Have fun doing that

William Davis

Ahh, you're great: gotta go for now

Maverick Ashley Lenartson

Thanks for the cumpliment

William Davis

I gotta go, ttyl

Maverick Ashley Lenartson

have a great evening...be kind to your self

William Davis

You as well, Sir!

Maverick Ashley Lenartson

Is that thumb going up my ass??? I sure hope so…

William Davis

No, it's my tongue, then it's my thumb

Maverick Ashley Lenartson

Open up that hole like only you can

William Davis

NAKED MEN thru facebook

I wish I could lick my own asshole...or suck my dick all the way to the base...

I sat on my face...and I farted but it was more than a fart...I had to stop the avalanche from coming out...so, I put a buttplug up there...

You have to ask yourself why you keep being mean to yourself: it's Ego related: you'll get an answer you may not like!

who wants to see me take off all my clothes and run down the street **NAKED**???

It's going to be a laugh fest, that's fer sher...

When somebody says, "Hi" to me why are they asking me if I'm high???

Don't ask me how I'm doing unless you have some really good drugs like weed, alcohol, food or you…

Why not have a good time all the time???

Why is it when I send naked pix of me to someone online they say, "You?" I say, "No, it's my brother."

I want to go to an orgy and be the center of all the attention and get cream pied

Emillio
You're hot
Maverick Ashley Lenartson
I'm hotter in person

Ronald Sinkler
You going to fuck me hard???
Maverick Ashley Lenartson
I'm going to fuck you so hard and cum in your ass. Then I'm going to tell you to push it out of your asshole and lick it up like an ice cream cone…

The Cocksuckers Association: who wants to join???

Hey there 'Orgy Boy', will you suck my dick off??? Give it to me now!

I live at **The Island of Forgotten Toys**

DeVos wants to change campus rules on sexual misconduct

Remember: a man or a woman can say, "He/She raped me," and you never laid a hand on that person or, maybe, you manhandled that person: manhandling a person is different from raping them as one is **BDSM** and the other is 'forcing your way into or on a person'...two separate ideas...be careful who you **sexually harass**...it could wind up being "downright dirty, dirty, dirty to the bone" w/ the "he said, she said" shite...it happened to me once: thank god the woman I was seeing at the time decided not to call the **Police** as I would have been in knee deep doo-doo and she's no longer my friend: she passed from "brain cancer" as she was susceptible to Cancer...not my fault...I got her to apologize in front of 3 people and she wouldn't look me in the eyes and that pissed me off even further but at least I got a "forced apology out of her" in front of people as I have no interest in "raping a 73 year older woman." It's not my style...

Fuck It Like It's Hot

Suck It Like It's Hot

Make Love To The Whole Wide World: nothing can bring you down ever!!!

What's your name: who's asking or Ha! Ha! Or Ha ha ha ha ha ha ha…

I don't need a Daddy as I am the Daddy: my names **Daddalicious**

Have a great evening everybody: time to get off facebook

why did the penis get limp? It was suffering from organ failure

IBM Card Wreaths For Veterans: 93.90 each: I'll give you a fun Blue or Red Lobstah Shirt just for buying the wreath for FREE: 34.60 values...that's a VALUE of 138.50 for 93.90 thanks so much...Happy Holidays...Gobble! Gobble!

John West

On a farm. Ok good, love it. Do you work on a farm or you bought the farm because you are a farmer? I dunno. Ha ha. John West I'm a farmer with my brothers. I love it. I don't do anything. I watch. I was an accident.

Why are pencils called colored pencils??? Because they like to make things colorful

'Come back dressed like a man.' Pastor recounts his confrontation with person dressed in 'drag' on Facebook Live.

I can't stop laughing: what is inappropriate dressing??? Hmm… Pastor Antonio Rocquemore of Power House International Ministries

I lost my hands from masturbating too much

I only jerk off one time a year and cover the whole nayborehood in snow…

No Christmas shopping for me: all I have to do is look thru my apartment and find stuff I don't want: it works like a charm…

My hole is twitching right now: I think it's going to suck your dick in…

What do you do when your hole twitches??? I wipe mine or scratch it…

What's your birth sign: mine's crazy

I put it in slowly like a turtle then I fuck like Bugs Bunny

Sounds like a triple orgasm: if you are a multiple-cummer

I'm related to Porky Pig right now butt eye'm ok w/ that…

How do you purse your lips??? I pull down my pants and spread my ass cheeks so you can get a very good look at my other mouth…be careful there are teeth in my asshole…

I'm in a relationship right now: I'm seeing my friend Doc Johnson: he really loves me and never says **NO**…or, "Honey, I've got a headache."

I was 4 lbs...in an incubator: no wonder your cock is so big: you got too much Oxygen...

He's between my legs right now: Mr Right Now...I'd rather use my cock pump butt eye don't know where I put him: he's like my friend Doc Johnson: he never disappears or says, "NO," or "Honey, I've got a headache." Always up for any challenges that cum his way. He is in competition w/ Doc Johnson and MR BUTTPLUG: they're going to give Maverick Ashleey Lenartson his Christmas Present early after he GET OFFS OFFLINE...

My next book: I Faggot - Maverick Ashleey Lenartson, Ph. D. in Pornography: I'm famous for being a writer and going to make some money at it on and offline this year and next year...PEACE & LOVE TO ALL MY FANS ON & OFFLINE: signed copies of my stories available just for you: shoot me an e-mail: ashleylenartson@gmail.com Thanks so much: I love all of you and want to fuck all of you for Christmas...https://tinyurl.com/cdvvejp Confessions of A Dirty Man Whore – Maverick Ashleey Lenartson: whore of the Century...I'm a famous Pornographer and I like my work...

I hope your day was a good one: it was so good: I bent over and sniffed my own arse and passed out from the stench of it...

Georgina Emily: where are you from??? my mother and father and I have no relatives to speak of: I'm Little Orphan Maverick Ashleey Lenartson, Baby I'm A Star

What's a Christmas pickle? The tradition you haven't heard of but will want to start now

I like to hide my micro-penis pickle in my Christmas Tree and whoever feels it first gets their 1st taste of Christmas and then the fistivities begin for the day and so much more: I'm so glad that I have a Christmas Pickle to put in my Dickmass Tree amongst the prickly branches...it suits my family just fine: Happy Christmas (War Is Over) - John Lennon & Yoko Ono...

Anal0Cowboy
The just fuck my pussy
Little Blo Peep
Your pussy needs to be fuct so hard by a hung guy and then there's a line of guys looking to get in there next: 50 guys dumping their hot steamy loads in your fuct out butthole...it never ends and you definitely can't walk after that! Every time you do another load seeps out of your well fuct hole!